Little Things

Abdellatif Laâbi

Translated from the French by Alan Baker

Leafe Press

Published by Leafe Press
www.leafepress.com
Nottingham, England.

This sequence of poems was originally published in 1992 as
'Les Petites Choses' and was included in the collecton 'Le
Soleil se Meurt' by La Différence, 103, Rue La Fayette, 75010
Paris. © La Différence.

This translation was published with the kind permission of
Abdellatif Laâbi.

Translation copyright © Alan Baker, 2013
Introduction copyright © Alan Baker, 2013

ISBN 978-0-9574048-3-0

Contents

Introduction

Abellatif Laâbi's native language is Arabic, but he was educated in French, the language of the colonial power in Morroco. Laâbi only learned to read and write Arabic in his thirties, when he was being held as a prisoner of conscience by the Morrocan regime; his powerful and moving prison correspondence, mainly addressed to his wife and children, is written in French (and published as "Chroniques de la citadelle d'exil"). In a recent interview (1), when asked why he continued to write in French, Laâbi answered "... the language in which a writer writes is either his mother tongue or the language that was imposed on him at some point because history wanted it." In the same interview, referring to his autobiographical novel, "Au fond de la jarre" (The Bottom of the Jar) he says "One of the concerns of 'The Bottom of the Jar' is a linguistic concern. In that book I tried to perfectly map the French language onto the Arabic language." So we have a writer who is acutely aware of different linguistic registers, and consequently capable of using a wide variety of tones. Laâbi's style ranges from the grand sweep of his surrealist-inspired narrative poems, which sometimes parody scriptural language, to the witty and epigrammatic tone of "Little Things". This latter style has been under-represented in English, and this is why I chose to translate this sequence, which is published here in English for the first time. "Little Things" (Les Petites Choses) was the fourth section of Laâbi's collection "Le Soleil se Meurt" published in 1992. The rest of that collection was included, in English translation, in "The World's Embrace", published by City Lights Books, which was the first extensive selection of Laâbi's work in English. "Little Things" employs an epigrammatic and gnomic tone, and its references to Sufism imply that it is both a homage to and a parody of that aspect of Islamic thought, with its elements of mysticism, tolerance and compassion (in a similar manner, Laâbi's long poem "Fragments of a Forgotten Genesis" references the tone of the Koran and the Christian Old Testament). But there is also a modernist and existential aspect to "Little Things", and the tension between this and the Islamic elements is one of the strengths of the sequence.

Alan Baker

1. Interview with Abdellatif Laâbi by Christopher Schaefer — Published on June 11, 2013 in "The Quarterly Conversation".

Little Things

The pen
ceased to obey
or dictate
It decided to be frivolous

It knows
about backlash
about disorder
and faint weariness of soul

It said to itself:
Why resist
the thing that betrays language
in order to make it more truthful?

The little things
will perhaps be
the big things of tomorrow
or yesterday

Example:
What deadly question
will be put to me by the Sphinx
who is
my travelling companion?

Example:
The station clock
Does it tell today's time,
or that of a day
a thousand years ago?

Example:
That man -
is he searching for a resting place
or for his passion in life?

The train moves off
Does it know the way?
Or if it will ever stop again?

The green of the fields
has absorbed all the colours
Hardly paying lip-service
to the poppy's red

The cows
graze dutifully
They're preparing
our future meals

A sickly cloud
lower than the others
Even the sky
has its lame ducks

Ah, that insolent barge
It openly does what it likes
to the water's fleece

The trees'
praise for the river
never runs dry

Water
begets love
but doesn't boast about it

More rare
the separation
the birds
are more rare

O lyrical bridges
the rivers exist
only for you

Koblenz
and its cruel station
It deserved
better perhaps

Some furnish their wait
Others prefer it bare

It's pretty
"thanks"
in whatever language

The man
bent over his vegetable patch
Lightning
of eternity

From the ruins
they have built an unfailing city
But in them
the cracks remain

If all these trees
joined hands
they would hold back the desert

Seize life
but don't exhaust it

Far
Far from what?
Each city
cradle
or grave
Each country
a language
in which love
stutters

Above the bed
is Christ
He smiles
sleeping
with his arms wide

Mankind
had a lucky streak
building mosques
Memory of Istanbul

Airport
The privileged stroll around
on the sanitized mirror-floor
There is dirt and more dirt!

Abidjan-Treichville
Black-white night
The dance-virus
cures all rheumatism

Why did the camel
come to Heidelberg?
To drink
in the Neckar of course!

A dogmatic
hotel room
Modern-day
nomad's tent

A southern man
bothers
the northern Sun

The night
discovers the town
It discovers her legs
her thighs
and little by little
the rest

Enough
of comparing towns
to women!

The look
kills
and resurrects

She saw it from the territories
the earth
She travels ticketless
within us

The other language
irritating
and longed-for
How can I say to it
take me
as if I spoke you?

The sun
resigns itself to the clouds
It has lost its appetite

Summer rain
The trees are grieving

The look
foresaw
the unforeseen

What advice
can the night offer
The night so devoid
of wisdom

The world warms
in the palm of the hand

The train lost its way
It was carrying a poet.

The bitter taste of coffee
The day begins
The millionth cigarette of the condemned man

The books sleep
leaning against each other
They're dreaming of the time of forests

It writes
from right to left
from left to right
It's called migratory language

Who's the phone ringing for
Wrong number
Or the long-awaited voice?

Sometimes
yes
you get weary
even of your passion

He keeps an eye out for the postman
hastily opens the mail
He's no longer afraid of deceptions

A letter
so rare
it says it's rarity
is what we've been waiting for

The unexpected:
everyone likes that
But look,
we make plans to schedule it

Silence
sculpts words
It has suicidal tendencies

When objects speak
we don't believe them
Then the ashtray rebels
the pen whines
the scissors are menacing
the glass closes over
the paper-knife hides a smirk
only the spectacles
maintain an air of detachment

The shelf said:
I feel
like a diverted aircraft

The circumcision chair said:
sadness keeps me company

The TV said:
I am the opium of the people
And I can't do anything about it.

The calendar said:
I bear not one cross
but many

The pebble said:
I was weaned
too young from sea

The portrait of the father said:
In a hundred years
I will still be here

The amber necklace said:
When will I wrap myself
around the neck
of the princess of my dreams?

The Linguaphone English course said:
I know my imperfections well

The manuscript said:
I must take out life insurance

The cigarette butt said:
I have already
settled my account with death

The cushion said:
I'm fed up with lazing around
I need the embrace of lovers

The cigarette lighter said:
Don't throw me away
I'm not biodegradable

The lamp said:
I don't like this unfair competition
from the day

The rain said:
Call the poet-friend
Surprise him with your tenderness

The Zemmour carpet said:
Be on your way
The country is eternal

Objects speak
the cup too
The scribe nods his head
and complies

Naked
in her bed
She touches herself
thinking of her lover
Her breasts already swelling
with millk

Garden perfumed
with the smell of flourishing bodies

- I want you
- You want what from me?
- What you haven't yet given

Mint tea
At the third glass
Nostalgia sits down in front of him
and takes away the taste

Her eyes shine
and run scared
She gives and takes back
in the same instant

What exactly are we hiding
when we say:
Let's talk frankly?

She passes
and the Atlantic swell
swirls around her waist
Her buttocks dethrone the Taj Mahal
Sirens sound in Paris

Instead of opening a mango
with a knife
why not try
a caress?

Prayer is better than sleep
shout the muezzins
Isn't sleep also a prayer?

The lover burning for his love
wants to offer her a serenade
but the much-desired
has had the unfortunate notion
of living on the ground floor

In the queue,
the long, long queue,
he sees those in front of him
as his enemies
and those behind him
as no-hopers

In the metro
even the most elegant
are poorly shod

On the park bench
they kiss methodically
When they do it in films
it's more real

As for women:
They always ask for a light
Never can find their keys
Furiously defend
the mess in their handbags

As for men:
They walk gracelessly
Hands in pockets
Turn up to gatherings
as if to a barracks.

Friend
or are we that in our youthful dreams?
We wanted to surprise the world
It surprised us

Since the world
is made like that
our dreams will have to be
even more stubborn

The round loaf
is easier to share

Wave
respects wave
The sand that welcomes them
shows no favouritism

Let our anxieties
be serene

Fear
is bad counsellor

The infinite
is in us
In fact
we are its source

God
is a paradox
It could be said that he fixes things
so that we can get by without him

He who sows stars
reaps peace

The country
makes itself wait
The lover
has learned patience

One day
Destiny will click its fingers
The wall, over there, will collapse
and the sceptics will say:
There, you see?

There will be
anarchy among the roses
perplexity in the desert
a wave in the soul's river
Women
will be on the march

Some children
will be born without sadness
but they won't know it

Where
must he begin
Washing words
or gardening the soul?

O night
don't be so zealous
Can't you see
we're worn out?

It's not
that we prefer the dawn to you
We feel for it in its chains
that's all

We will pass away
having been crazy about life
Did we really mind?

Yet
everything encouraged us
to be eternal

What follies
still-born
in this trick of time

Have our wisdoms
bribed us?

Article censored
from the Declaration:
Each man has the right
to a life of catching up

Everything reverts to order
or disorder
It's all the same

Message
no message
Tentative trail
before the ride
of the next lot of barbarians

What fun
your testaments are!

The woman at home
is well worth
the man at home

How would one explain
make-believe to masculine logic?

Invisible work
secret offering

The nomad dreams of a house
The house-dweller of a camel
Siamese dreams

That which separates
the earth and sky
and which connects them:
a man drawn up
to his full height.

If we really listen
to music,
it will listen to us.

The sufi knows
that he speaks of carnal love
His art consists
in making others speak of it

Sufi's self-criticism:
I admit it
My submission engendered pride
My love lusted for power

Next, from the self-critique:
O my eyes
do you open to the absence of love
or do you close so that a child
could take me by the hand
and help me to cross

My brothers, sorry,
I've neglected your concerns
about water
about the baton
and about bread

I didn't realise
that wool, of which my tunic is made,
is expensive nowadays

Conclusion:
I didn't realise
that my usefulness
resides in my lack of usefulness
I sought health
there, where it isn't

The confession of the sufi
torments the profane poet
He says to himself:
Who speaks thus
in him
in me?

In my heart
his eye or mine?

I circle around him
He circles around me
No mirror separates us

He convinces me of essence
I convince him of appearances

He troubles me with his certainty
I trouble him with my doubt

His exile is a promise
My exile a quest

Him
or me
who is the heretic?
who is the believer?

Goodbye sufi
concluded the profane poet
our meeting was brief
and tempting

Garden conforming to childhood
Its mineral trees
Its fossil fruits
The wound where the spring disappears

Because he was small
the world was big
Rumour flowed
through the fountains

Dawn a song
dusk a litany
Midday burned his fingers
around the table

The face was in
its soft-authoritarian place
and when its mouth opened
God spoke humbly

Today's tears
are crafty by comparison

From bread
there wasn't a crumb too much

Water rests
in the jar
like pearls in a safe

Questions germinate in silence
and feed on it

That child is no more
Perhaps at the moment of goodbye
he will come back
to hum a shared lullaby
to the dying

Death is watchful
as is life

The friend
who we deserted
has just become
as old as the world

What is more concrete
than death?
What is more abstract?

The child plays
in all seriousness
Ah, if only he could cheat
like an adult!

Dark craftsman
in the dark workshop
in the dark country
Picasso of silence

Stay to write
the eulogy of the bed
The dictionary of disappointed ideas

How delicious the word is
after long silence!

Grains of laughter
to cultivate
in the thankless field of masks

Laughing brother
or as we say
foster brother

His double appeared
and dropped behind him
and called him
- Hey you
What! Me?
Where are you coming from?
Where are we going?

There is no compass
that will point to where love is

One day we should
apologize to the earth
and tiptoe quietly away

Select Bibliography

In addition to his poetic oeuvre, Laâbi has published novels, autobiography, drama, children's books and many translations from Arabic into French. What follows is a select bibliography, of Laâbi's poetry, and of English translations of his work.

Poetry

1. Le Règne de barbarie. Seuil, Paris (épuisé). 1980.
2. Histoire des sept crucifiés de l'espoir. La Table rase, Paris. 1980.
3. Sous le bâillon le poème. L'Harmattan, Paris. 1981.
4. Discours sur la colline arabe. L'Harmattan, Paris, 1985.
5. L'Écorché vif. L'Harmattan, Paris. 1986.
6. Tous les déchirements. Messidor, Paris. 1990.
7. Le soleil se meurt. La Différence, Paris. 1992.
8. L'Étreinte du monde. La Différence, Paris. 1993.
9. Le Spleen de Casablanca. La Différence, Paris. 1996.
10. Poèmes périssables, La Différence, coll. Clepsydre, Paris. 2000.
11. L'automne promet, La Différence, coll. Clepsydre, Paris. 2003.
12. Les Fruits du corps, La Différence, coll. Clepsydre, Paris. 2003.
13. Œuvre poétique, La Différence, coll. Œuvre complète, Paris. 2003
14. Écris la vie, La Différence, coll. Clepsydre, Paris. 2005.
15. Mon cher double, La Différence, coll. Clepsydre, Paris. 2007.
16. Tribulations d'un rêveur attitré, coll. La Clepsydre, La Différence, Paris. 2008.
17. Oeuvre poétique II, La Différence. 2010.

Laâbi in English

1. Rue du Retour (Le Chemin des ordalies, roman), translated by Jacqueline Kaye, Readers Intenational, Londres, 1989
2. The World's Embrace (selected poems), translated by Anne George, Edris Makward, Victor Reinking and Pierre Joris, City Lights Books, San 3. Francisco,2003
4. Fragments of a forgotten genesis, translated by Nancy Hadfield and Gordon Hadfield, Leafe Press, Nottingham, UK, 2009
5. The Jackal's Baptism (Le Baptême chacaliste, théâtre), translated by Gordon and Nancy Hadfield, Mayday Magazine, Ontario (Canada), 2010
6. The Rule of Barbarism (Le Règne de Barbarie, poésie) translated by André Naffis-Sahely, Island Position (Brooklyn - Gorée- Maastricht), 2012
7. The Bottom of the Jar (Le Fond de la jarre, roman) translated by André Naffis-Sahely, Archipelago Books (New York, Etats-Unis), 2013

www.ingramcontent.com/pod-product-compliance
Lightning Source LLC
LaVergne TN
LVHW051202080426
835508LV00021B/2756